# SUBJECTS LACKING WORDS?

## THE GRAY ZONE OF THE GREAT FAMINE

BREANDÁN MAC SUIBHNE

This essay is part of the interdisciplinary series *Famine Folios*, covering many aspects of the Great Hunger in Ireland from 1845–52.

# CONTENTS

# IN MEMORIAM

Maisie (née Kennedy) O'Keefe (1930–2016), Cappry, County Donegal, Ireland and New Haven, Connecticut, United States of America, and her mother, Maggie (née Kennedy) Gardiner (1904–83), Tullybeg, County Donegal, Ireland and Wallasey, Merseyside, England

*T*heir conversations then were not as in the years long and not long past – not of wars, not of battles, nor the strength of nations; no, their subjects were lacking words, more silent, [and of a] more mournful nature.

It was a rehearsal of their own sad experience of the past few years – the silence, the sadness, the desolation around ... the recollection of the immense population at one time, and their dispersion almost unawares.

Hugh Dorian, 1890

Figure 1 | Irish School, *Lest We Forget*

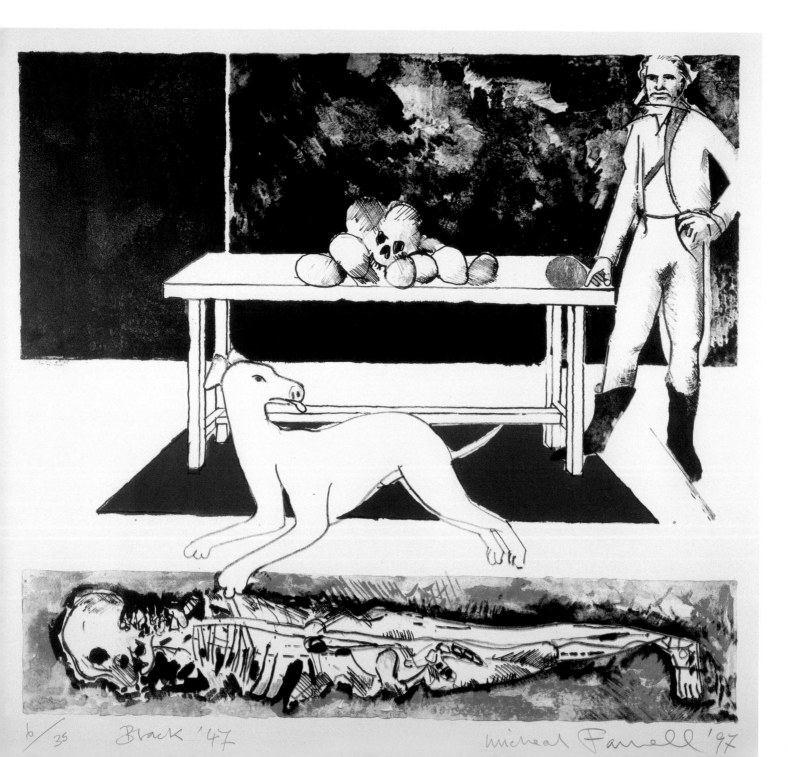

6/35    Black '47                    Micheal Farrell '97

# REDUCTION

It was, he thought, "as if the grave had that moment vomited her forth". It was Friday January 22, 1847, cold and wet, with a gale rising. Her married name was Keating. She was from Letter, two miles outside Skibbereen. And she had "crawled" those two miles to the house of Daniel Donovan, a thirty-nine-year-old dispensary doctor, on North Street. She was suffering from "malignant fever" and "emaciated to the utmost degree", and Donovan, though a compassionate man, was afraid that she would infect his own young family. He handed her a shilling and told her to leave his door.

"I don't want this," she said of the doctor's shilling, "but I want to get my boy buried; he is dead these eleven days, he died in two days after his father; I got the sickness myself; my two children are dying; no person will go to give them or me a drink of the cold water, and I got up in the fever today and put the corpse in a ditch, and I came to you to get it put in the grave, that the dogs may not eat it."

That evening Donovan and Jerry Crowley, the town apothecary, went out to Letter. The "scene of misery" appalled them:

*The mud floor of the hovel was one mass of filth, the rain pouring down freely through the rotten thatch; on the ground, which was a perfect* cloaca *[sewer], lay two children upon whose bodies the anatomy of the bones could be studied as perfectly as on a dried skeleton; and in the ditch in front of the door was a coffin, containing the putrid body of a dead boy of seven years old.*

Donovan asked the woman how she had procured the coffin. She told him that it was the shilling that he had given her to buy food that paid for it. Neither she nor her other two children, she said, "cared about the victuals now, as they forgot the taste of them".

Donovan and Crowley began to dig a grave in the corner of a "kitchen garden", a vegetable patch. None of the woman's neighbors came near them. And so they

**Figure 2** | Micheal Farrell, *Black '47*

finished the grave, "or rather the hole", as Crowley phrased it, alone, and there they buried the seven-year-old boy who had been eleven days dead in that hovel with his mother and siblings.[1]

It was eleven o'clock that night when they got back to Skibbereen. Four days later, on Tuesday January 26, Donovan was going up High Street to attend a family in fever. Someone caught him by the coat, and turning around he recognized the Widow Keating. She had come into town to bury her daughter, Mary, who had died the previous morning. But she had something else on her mind. "Doctor," she said, "won't you send for my boy? The pigs got into the field where you put him, and I fear they will root the grave, and as no Christian would come near me, I brought in little Mary myself to lay her alongside of her father in the Chapel-yard."

Donovan hired two men to remove the coffined corpse of the seven-year-old from the garden and reinter it in consecrated ground. However, on going out to Letter they found that the body of the boy, then over two weeks dead, was "in such an advanced state of decomposition as not to admit of its being raised by them". The next day the Widow Keating herself exhumed the putrid corpse, brought it into Skibbereen, and buried it with the remains of her husband and daughter.

Seven days later, on Tuesday February 2, the widow again met Donovan in the street and "accosted" him with "a demand for another coffin for the last of her children and family, who was then lying dead". She perceived a certain hesitation on his part – he had already purchased coffins for two of her children, and contributed towards the burial of her husband. And so she implored him "in the name of the great God, not to let her fine boy, that would be her help and support if he lived, be thrown into the grave like a dog" [Figure 3].

"There was something so impressive in the manner and so awe-inspiring in the death-like appearance of this spectre-looking woman", wrote Donovan, now calling her Mrs Keating, "that I yielded to her entreaties; the coffin was purchased; she placed it on her head, and was about to leave the town when I again saw her. I remonstrated with this dying creature, who was during the whole of these melancholy scene[s] labouring under famine-fever, and pointed out the risk that would attend her undertaking such a task in her weakly state."

But the Widow Keating disregarded his advice, and walked home with the "heavy coffin" on her head. She reached her cabin door, fell to the ground before entering it, and died "a victim", as Donovan put it, "to her fondness for her family, and reverential respect for their remains".

In Letter, Keating's neighbors, dreading contagion, would not go near her body, and so it lay outside her cabin door until the next day, when Donovan heard of her fate and sent a car for her remains and those of her son. He had the two of them laid with her husband, her daughter, Little Mary, and her other son "to sleep in death with those whom she had so much loved in life". And he promised himself that when he had time he would have a headstone raised to this "martyr to maternal duty", this "humble heroine", so that,

> *Her sad tale shall one speaking stone declare*
> *From future eyes to draw a pitying tear.*[2]

**Figure 3** | Rowan Gillespie, *Famine*

CLD CHAPEL-LANE, SKIBBEREEN.

Figure 4 | James Mahony, "Old Chapel-Lane"

Daniel Donovan was to live another thirty years. It is not known if he ever raised that stone. Today no monument to the Keatings of Letter – the father who died on January 9, the mother who died on February 2, and their three children who died between those dates – can be found in Skibbereen. Yet, through the doctor's account, the Widow Keating's determination, *in extremis*, to see her children buried with some semblance of decency, her clutching at that which marks us out as human, survives the wreck of time. And so, too, does the doctor's compassion. But no less conspicuous is the refusal of her neighbors to assist in the removal and interment of her dead.

That refusal shook Donovan as it did Crowley, who remarked on it in a letter to a friend in Cork. Yet it is difficult to judge those neighbors. Malignant typhoid fever, which extinguished that starving family, was highly contagious. Indeed, two leading physicians would later calculate that in the year 1847 alone 131 Irish medical men succumbed to "epidemic and contagious disease", with the vast majority (123) dying of fever. It is an extraordinary toll in a single year of a more protracted crisis on a profession that numbered some 2,600 male practitioners, and it is all the more extraordinary as it excludes women working as matrons and nurses (Froggat 134–56).[3] Donovan himself later remarked of west Cork "that almost every person actively engaged in the administration of relief to the poor was attacked with fever". And he gave one striking example of its transmissibility:

*A poor man ... came to my house (with a crowd of others) to look for soup-tickets. His weak state attracted the attention of a strong robust woman, a neighbour of mine, who caught him by the shoulder for the purpose of directing my attention to his case; she instantly complained of the offensive smell from his body, had rigors that night, and was dead of malignant low typhoid fever within five days.[4]*

And so the neighbors' refusal of assistance to the Widow Keating (the refusal even to dig a hole) – like Donovan's initial concern that his family might contract fever from her – can be explained. Moreover, many, although not necessarily all, of those neighbors were doubtless also in a dire condition. In 1851 the population of Letter (properly Lettertinlish) was 106 persons – sixty males and forty-six females – exactly half of what it had been in 1841 (212 persons). And there was then exactly half the number of inhabited houses, seventeen, where a decade earlier there had been thirty-four. And much of this winnowing of men, women, and children – by death, migration, and committal to the poorhouse – would have taken place in the three months before and four or five months after January 1847, when Daniel Donovan found the Widow Keating, as if the grave had vomited her, at his door.[5]

Another mother, in another place, in January 1847 provides another example of moral conflicts in a time of famine. Just before Christmas 1846 the wife of Robert Shane gave birth when staying with her parents, Robert and Anne Curran, at Creevy, near Shankill, County Down; on December 26 her husband returned to their own house, taking with him an older daughter, Margaret Jane, aged two years and four months, leaving his wife and the newborn with the Currans. On the evening of Sunday January 3, Shane, who had been reduced to begging, brought the child back to his in-laws' place. Anne O'Brien, a lodger, heard a knocking at the door, and then the little girl crying and "frequently" calling out "Granny, granny, let me in!" But the grandmother would not open the door, and Shane was ordered about his business by Robert Curran: "he had told him to go out of that with his child". Shane, she said, could be heard outside telling the child "Call ma, and call granny", and the child was heard to say "Da, take me away; granny won't let us in." The child's own mother, according to O'Brien, did not rise when she heard her call. "The wretched man", it was reported, "then took away the rejected child, of whom he was very fond; and soon after [three days later] the helpless being was found dead in a field [belonging to Curran]." She was dressed and wearing a little bonnet; it had been snowing, and she was lying face down in an inch or two of water. Dr Robert Kelso, who conducted a post-mortem examination, judged that the child had been two or three days dead, likely having perished from the cold; she had eaten something two or three hours before her death.

Robert Shane was charged with the murder of his daughter by exposing her to the inclemency of the weather. At his trial, which heard that his in-laws were not in want, an attorney who had volunteered to represent him deplored the "outrage to natural impulses done by the mother and grandmother of the child" who had not admitted her to the house when she called out to them. The Currans, he said, were "a very feelingless, heartless set". Shane had come to their house "in a state of starvation, hoping, at least, that his child would be saved from the horrors of starvation, after having shared with it his last crust, for it was proved by the coroner that the child had aliment in its stomach". In charging the jury, Chief Justice John Doherty recommended a merciful view of the case:

*If that parent, going from door to door to seek relief, and, perhaps, wearied with carrying his infant, had left it where he thought it might be safest, intending to return, and if on his return, he found that it had perished whilst he was away seeking help for it, the merciful spirit of our laws throws a shield around him, and his conduct is not to be condemned as murder.*

The jury convicted Shane of manslaughter. Sentencing him to six months' hard labour, Doherty told him that he had been ably defended by counsel, "but he had a still better advocate in the conscience of every man who heard the case". And, with what the *Downpatrick Recorder* described as "indignant eloquence", he vehemently deplored the hard-hearted conduct of the mother and grandmother.[6]

The late 1840s produced numerous other incidents involving the abandonment of family members: indeed, poorhouses were crowded with deserted wives and children and the unwanted elderly. Yet some cases admit of no easy judgement: in February 1847, an inquest near Kenmare, County Kerry on the body of Ellen Connor heard that she had gone with her husband to Owen Sullivan's house for a night's lodging; she had collapsed "from exhaustion" before reaching the house; her husband fetched Sullivan; being "unable" to bring her inside, they left her where she lay, and the following morning found her dead. Rebuked by the coroner for not remaining with his wife, the husband had retorted, "Perhaps your worship will tell me what better thing could happen her", adding that his only regret was that he did not remain outside himself and perish with her.[7]

Refusal to assist persons in distress, including the abandonment of dependants, seems only slightly less grievous than deliberately inflicting harm on a person. And in the years of the Famine, poor people did inflict harm on persons similarly circumstanced to themselves, often by stealing small supplies of food: houses and hovels were burgled, hungry people were waylaid coming home from shops and soup kitchens, and bread was snatched from the hands of the starving. Indeed, people murdered for food. One horrific incident occurred outside Rosscarbery, west Cork in spring 1847. Men employed on the public works used to go to nearby houses to boil their breakfasts. On the morning of March 4, Denis Finn of Carhoogarriff and his twelve-year-old son Johnny took their breakfast in Corran, in the house of Judith Donoghue. She was living with three children – Johnny (14), Mary (*c.* 6–7), and Jerry (4) – her husband having died on the first Tuesday in Lent, February 23. The Finns – who lived only about two miles away – had been breakfasting with her for nine or ten days. After the Finns had left that morning, the widow took Johnny with her to get soup in exchange for turf from Rev. Richard Hayes, the rector, at Ballyroe; the soup was not ready when they arrived and so she sent the boy home. There he found Jerry dead, face down near the door, and Mary dead on her back in the corner near the fireplace. Their throats had been cut with the widow's own knife, which was found under Mary's "poll" (back of the head); Judith would later say that "her head had been cut off all to a little bit of the poll behind", and Jerry's throat cut from ear to ear. Missing was a small gray bag of oatmeal flour that the widow had locked in a box with a cake of bread she had made that morning; the box was now in pieces on the floor. Also missing was a pair of shoes belonging to the widow's late husband.[8]

Eight days later Johnny Finn was arrested in the poorhouse in Skibbereen. Philip Somerville, a magistrate, with Constable Michael Jordan translating from the Irish, took a statement from the child, who spoke no English:

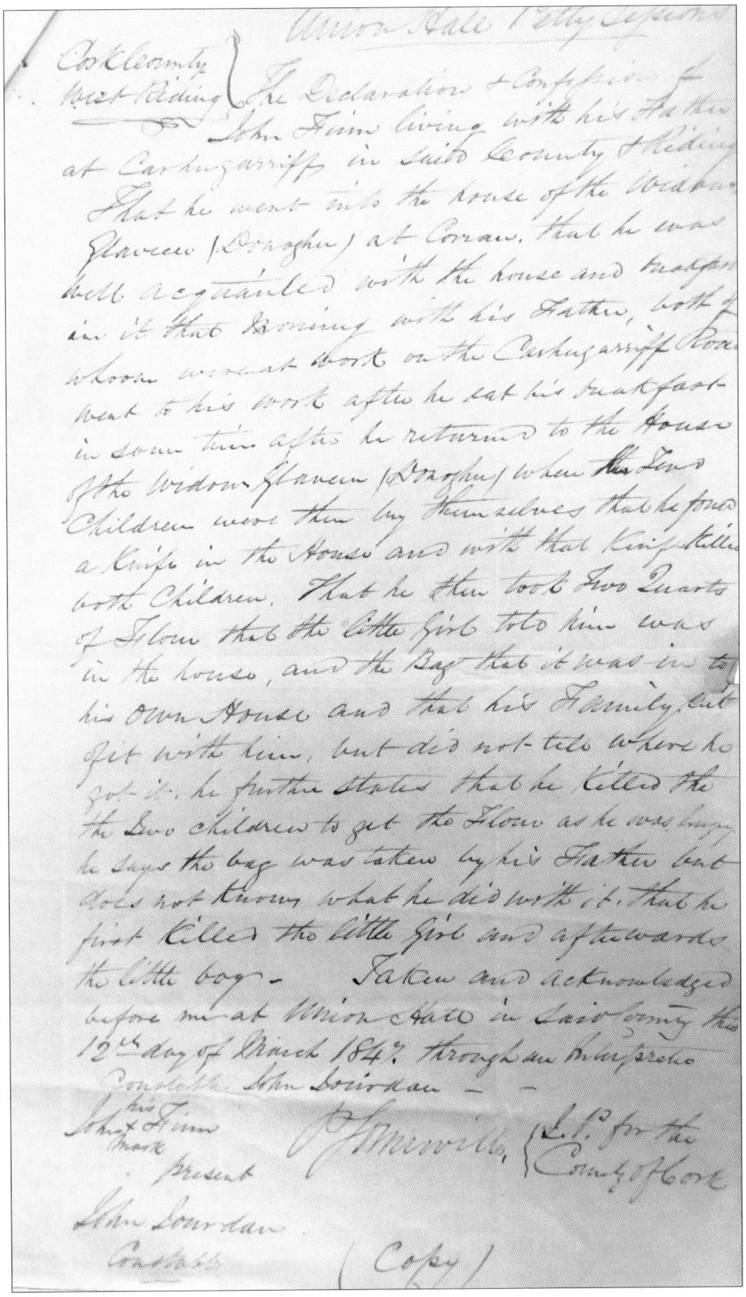

**Figure 5 | Image of confession of Johnny Finn**

*... the two children were then by themselves; that he found a knife in the house and with that knife killed both children. That he took two quarts of flour that the little girl told him was in the house and the bag that it was in to his own house and that his family eat of it with him, but [he] did not tell where he got it; he further states that he killed the two children to get the flour, as he was hungry ... he first killed the little girl and afterwards the little boy* **[Figure 5]**.

"He is a most wretched-looking half-starved creature", Somerville remarked when forwarding this confession to Dublin, "and what to do with him I am at a loss to know".[9]

Finn's first trial, in April 1848, collapsed when a juror took ill. That July he was acquitted of murder, his attorney having, inter alia, created a reasonable doubt as to whether the "emaciated" child – who he claimed had been only ten in spring 1847 – had the physical power to kill the Donoghues; he also strongly imputed the double murder to his father, Denis, who that morning had asked the widow "what she gave for the meal or did she bring much of it [from market]". The general impression in the court, according to the *Dublin Evening Packet*, was that the verdict was a proper one.[10] But others entertained no doubts about Johnny Finn's capacity to kill. Before the case had even come to trial, Daniel Donovan had given his opinion of the boy:

*... he subsequently was admitted into the Skibbereen Workhouse, and then frankly admitted his act to me; did not consider that he was guilty of any crime; did not think that he deserved or would suffer any penalty for it; the unfortunate being appeared so stolid and dull that I thought he must be a congenital idiot; but on making inquiry into his previous history, I ascertained that he was a boy of great cunning, and always regarded as an artful, designing knave.*

*Since he was committed to jail, and received a sufficient supply of food, his faculties have again brightened; and I was lately informed by one of the officers of the prison that he is regarded as the most artful rogue in the entire establishment; and altogether denies any knowledge of the murders, which he before admitted were perpetrated by him.*[11]

Within five years of the boy's acquittal, there was no Finn householder in Carhoogarriff. Unless she had remarried, the Widow Donoghue had no house of her own in Corran,[12] and the daughter of Rev. Richard Hayes, to whose house she had gone that fateful morning for soup, was dead from typhoid fever.[13]

If conditions in west Cork were particularly atrocious in early 1847, when the Donoghue children were murdered, other places and periods during the Famine witnessed no-less-appalling incidents involving poor people killing and being killed for food. Indeed, as at Corran, it was sometimes children or elderly people left minding a small supply of meal who were the victims. For instance, on April 1, 1847, less than a month after the murder of the Donoghues, Mary Hegarty, a seventy-five-year-old widow, was murdered at Castletown, about a mile and a half from

**Figure 6** | Brian Maguire, *The World is Full of Murder* [Detail]

Ballycastle, County Mayo. She had been left alone when some family members went to the shore "for the purpose of gathering seaweed for food", and another had gone to Ballycastle "to get some soup". Knowing that the Hegartys had a "small bag of meal", a local boy, James Sweeney, aged about fourteen, determined to rob it, and, in the process or to prevent discovery, he inflicted six or seven wounds with a loy (heavy spade) on the "old and feeble woman" and left her to die "weltering in her gore".[14] And a fortnight later, in the same county, on April 15, 1847, a "poor man" named Michael Lavelle, of Tallagh, Erris, went with his wife to the fair in Belmullet, leaving their twelve-year-old nephew, Patrick Dixon, at home. On their return "they found the boy quite dead, prostate inside the door; a spade lay at his feet, a tongs beside him, both covered with his blood and hair and the house robbed of the only provisions the[y] had, about a stone of meal, a little rice, and two haddock". Suspicion fell on a fellow of about seventeen or eighteen years of age named Michael Mullowney, who "bore a bad character". He, too, was a nephew of Michael Lavelle.[15]

Not surprisingly, then, there was a sharp understanding in the 1840s that the effects of extreme want are not simply physical. "Alas", Michael Enright, the parish priest of Bonane and Glengarriff, wrote to the bishop of Kerry, in February 1847,

*what a mighty change has come over my poor people within the short space of four months. I can no longer recognize them, physically or morally. Their bodies are worn down to mere skeletons, and their deeds! their daily and nightly depredations! make me fear that their very souls are tainted and demoralized by the ghastly Demon of hunger!!!*[16]

Enright, in decrying "demoralization", was primarily concerned about "depredations" – theft. And that concern owed something to the burgling of his own house: on January 14 some people had broken into it and taken food intended for the priest's use and for the relief of his parishioners.[17] Daniel Donovan expressed a fuller understanding of the "moral" consequences of hunger and disease. "The most singular effect produced by the horrors of the famine now raging", he wrote in January 1847, "is the severance of the ties of consanguinity which it has caused, and the destruction which it has induced of the ardent domestic affections that formed, perhaps, the strongest trait in the character of the Irish peasant." He had been particularly struck by an incident in his dispensary:

*A woman named Driscoll came to get medicine for her husband, who was affected with road sickness; whilst I was prescribing for him, a woman, who entered the surgery, begged that I would give her something for a sick child; upon which the female first alluded to exclaimed, "Bad luck to them for children! I have five of them sick, and I would think myself lucky, if they were all dead before morning."*

Donovan remonstrated with that woman for her "apparent cruelty", but she persisted: "[T]his time twelve months I would as soon lose my heart's blood as one of my children, but it is killing me now to see them starving and crying."[18] And a year later, reflecting on the storm of death that had raged through his district, Donovan was even more insistent on the moral consequences of famine:

*Another symptom of starvation, and one that accounts for the horrible scenes that famine usually exhibits, is the total insensibility of the sufferers to every other feeling except supplying their own wants. I have seen mothers snatch food from the hands of their starving children; known a son to engage in a fatal struggle with a father for a potato; and have seen parents look on the putrid bones of their offspring without evincing a symptom of sorrow. Such is the inevitable consequence of starvation; and it is unfair to attribute to inherent faults in our people the moral degradation to which they are at present reduced, and which is inseparable from a state of severe physical privation.*[19]

Therein lies a brute reality of famine. It "reduces" people, pushes them below the waterline of what they had understood to be civilized behavior. And so the Widow Keating of Letter answers Diogenes the Cynic, who asked why it mattered if bodies were tossed over the city wall to be devoured by birds and beasts. Until the day that she died at her own door, having borne home a coffin for her third and last child, that remarkable woman affirmed that the care society accords its dead raises the living above the level of the dogs and pigs that would have devoured the bodies of her children.[20] She, who is numbered among the Famine dead, died undefeated.

# THE GRAY ZONE

In *The Drowned and the Saved* (1986), Primo Levi recalled the "brusque revelation" on entering Auschwitz that "hope of solidarity from one's companions in misfortune" was a grand delusion. The absence of that expected support

*became manifest from the very first hours of imprisonment, often in the instant form of a concentric aggression on the part of those in whom one hoped to find future allies … the first threats, the first insults, the first blows came not from the SS but from other prisoners, from "colleagues", from those mysterious personages who nevertheless wore the same striped tunic that they, the new arrivals, had just put on.*

The interior of the camp "could not be reduced to two blocs of victims and persecutors", not only because prisoners took advantage of each other, but also because some, for a variety of reasons, collaborated and received rewards and privileges from their captors. For Levi, this is the "gray zone", the space that separates victims and persecutors – one populated by obscene and pathetic Figures, where sometimes, but not always, judgement is impossible (20, 36–69). And in considering that moral space, he states the obvious: the saved "may not necessarily be the best, those predestined to do good, the bearers of a message", but "the selfish, the violent, the insensitive, the collaborators of the 'gray zone', the spies" (82).

The gray zone of the Great Famine[21] is the demi-monde of soupers and grabbers, moneylenders and meal-mongers, and those among the poor who had a full pot when neighbors starved, and the poorhouse bully who took the biscuit from the weak. It is where one finds the wife of Robert Shane, who denied one child food and fed another, and Johnny Finn (or his father), who slit the throats of two children for a bag of meal, and, indeed, cases of cannibalism, rumored and reported.[22] And for the historian, with only the barest bones to pick over, it is the moral space inhabited by the neighbors of the Widow Keating – people quite possibly related to her. To make these observations is not to be oblivious to what Margaret Kelleher has called the danger of drawing trite comparisons between the Famine and the Holocaust, nor is it to commit to any classification of the earlier horror. Rather, it is to acknowledge some issues raised

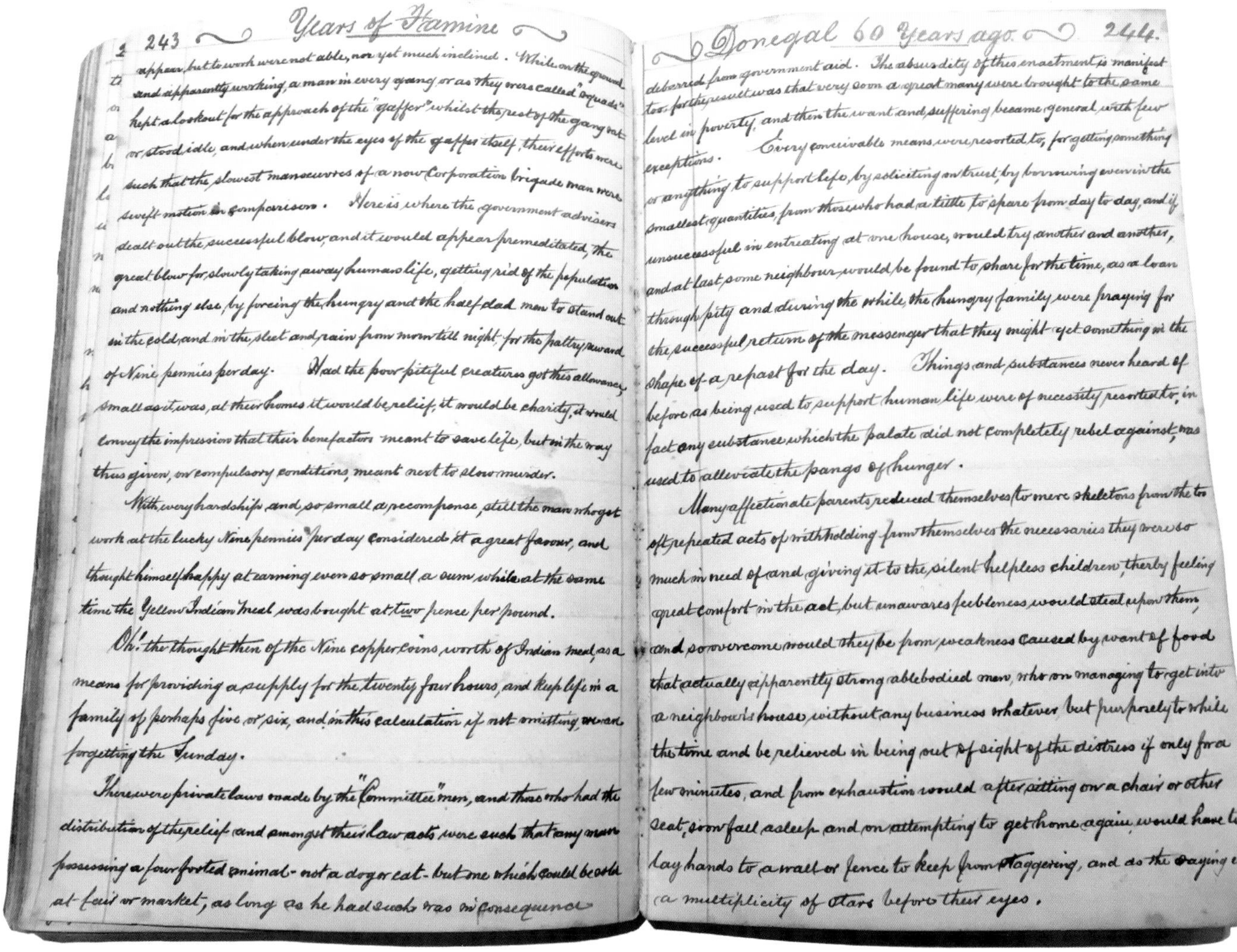

243 Years of Famine

appear, but to work were not able, nor yet much inclined. While on the ground
and apparently working, a man in every gang or as they were called "squads"
kept a lookout for the approach of the "gaffer" whilst the rest of the gang sat
or stood idle, and when under the eyes of the gaffer itself, their efforts were
such that the slowest manoeuvres of a now Corporation brigade man were
swift motion in comparison. Here is where the government advisers
dealt out the successful blow, and it would appear premeditated, the
great blow for slowly taking away human life, getting rid of the population
and nothing else, by forcing the hungry and the half dead men to stand out
in the cold, and in the sleet and rain from morn till night, for the paltry reward
of Nine pennies per day. Had the poor pitiful creatures got this allowance,
small as it was, at their homes it would be relief, it would be charity, it would
convey the impression that their benefactors meant to save life, but in the way
thus given, on compulsory conditions, meant next to slow murder.
With every hardships and so small a recompense, still the man who got
work at the lucky Nine pennies per day considered it a great favour, and
thought himself happy at earning even so small a sum, while at the same
time the Yellow Indian Meal was bought at two pence per pound.
Oh! the thought then of the Nine copper coins, worth of Indian meal, as a
means for providing a supply for the twenty four hours, and keep life in a
family of perhaps five or six, and in this calculation if not omitting, or and
forgetting the Sunday.
There were private laws made by the "Committee" men, and those who had the
distribution of the relief and amongst their law acts were such that any man
possessing a four footed animal - not a dog or cat - but one which could be sold
at fair or market, as long as he had such was in consequence

Donegal 60 Years ago. 244.

debarred from government aid. The absurdity of this enactment is manifest
too, for the result was that very soon a great many were brought to the same
level in poverty, and then the want and suffering became general, with few
exceptions. Every conceivable means were resorted to, for getting something
or anything to support life, by soliciting on trust, by borrowing even in the
smallest quantities, from those who had a little to spare from day to day, and if
unsuccessful in entreating at one house, would try another and another,
and at last some neighbour would be found to share for the time, as a loan
through pity and during the while, the hungry family were praying for
the successful return of the messenger that they might get something in the
shape of a repast for the day. Things and substances never heard of
before as being used to support human life were of necessity resorted to, in
fact any substance which the palate did not completely rebel against, was
used to alleviate the pangs of hunger.
Many affectionate parents reduced themselves to mere skeletons from the too
oft repeated acts of withholding from themselves the necessaries they were so
much in need of and giving it to the silent helpless children, thereby feeling
great comfort in the act, but unawares feebleness would steal upon them,
and so overcome would they be from weakness caused by want of food
that actually apparently strong ablebodied men, who on managing to get into
a neighbour's house, without any business whatever, but purposely to while
the time and be relieved in being out of sight of the distress if only for a
few minutes, and from exhaustion would after sitting on a chair or other
seat, soon fall asleep and on attempting to get home again, would have to
lay hands to a wall or fence to keep from staggering, and as the saying is
a multiplicity of stars before their eyes.

**Figure 7** | Hugh Dorian manuscript

by the condition to which ragged humanity was, in places, reduced in Ireland in the late 1840s, and to bring into view situations in which moral judgement may not then have been impossible but can scarcely have been easy, and today seems utterly inappropriate.

*

An awareness of the gray zone saturates Hugh Dorian's recollections of life and death in mid-nineteenth-century north Donegal **[Figure 7]**. Born on a smallholding in 1834, Dorian entered his teens in the years of the Famine, when more than one in four people in his wider community would be lost. And in 1889–90 he wrote of what he had seen. It was four decades since the Famine, about the same span between the Holocaust and the writing of *The Drowned and the Saved*. Dorian's memoir, if less calibrated and less consistent in judgement, and, in intellectual force and focus, less concentrated than Levi's, is no less the reflective testimony of a survivor of a horrendous calamity. And like the camp survivor in his earlier *If This Is a Man* (1947), the Famine survivor turns to the most fundamental issues: "The questions naturally arise, What is man? And, What is life? What can be the cause of all this? Is it a punishment for our crimes? Or those of our forefathers, or is it to purify souls here by suffering to prepare them for a happy eternity hereafter?" (Dorian 256)

Dorian was not uninterested in responsibility for the horror that he survived. Most of the time he simply thought it obvious where it lay. If he stops short of indicting the British state with premeditated mass murder – a charge made by some, but by no means all, nationalists and republicans – he still locates the suffering of those years in a long history of colonial oppression, the violence of which was inscribed in a landscape made up of the "rich lands of the plantation" and the "mountain, the bog and the seashore" inhabited by the "Celt". "The Donegal peasant has got all the historical learning he requires", he writes; "he has his ancestors' history open before him everyday he rises: it is exhibited in the large characters – the ocean, the mountain, and his own state of poverty – and if he reads anything he must read how it is that he is there and why" (130). Moreover, he does explicitly hold Britain to account for the calamity, identifying public works schemes as the point where the

*government advisers dealt out the successful blow – and it would* appear *premeditated – the great blow for slowly taking away human life, getting rid of the population and nothing else, by forcing the hungry and the half-clad men to stand out in the cold and in the sleet and rain from morn till night for the paltry reward of nine pennies per day. Had the poor pitiful creatures got this allowance, small as it was, at their homes, it would have been relief, it would be charity, it would convey the impression that their benefactors meant to save life, but in the way thus given, on compulsory conditions, it meant* next to *slow murder* (216–17).[23]

Crucially, this nationalist analysis frames a more intimate history. At times, indeed, Dorian's voice rings out of the gray zone:

*Arising from death, emigration, and dispersion to all parts, the population soon dwindled away. And indeed I hope it will not be any way uncharitable to say [it, but] with the multitude also disappeared many turbulent and indifferent characters who were only a disgrace to the good, the honest and the well-doing, and if there was poverty, there was peace too* (223).

These words are all the more unsettling as Dorian himself drank and brawled through his adult years, and on a night in late December 1899, his wife Catherine fell into the River Foyle in Derry and drowned; she had just been released from a constabulary barracks on the Strand Road – having been arrested for public drunkenness – to get somebody to fetch their daughter, who had been arrested with her (41–3). And if an "uncharitable" attitude to the loss of some rougher members of his own community disturbs Dorian's clear conviction that Britain was responsible – in the long term and the short – for the tragedy that befell Ireland, so, too, does a grasping at providential explanations of hunger and disease, death and migration:

*Were we permitted to moralize we would say that the Almighty in His wise ways has brought about dispersions, emigrations and deaths as a punishment upon the people, as they were too numerous, too unruly, and in their ways of life ... too rebellious; therefore, a Higher Power was needed to curb and to chastise them. Emigration thinned their ranks. Starvation reduced them to weakness, and deaths thinned and decimated their ranks worst of all, but it gave the remainder, though few, a chance of thinking for themselves (172–3).*

In Dorian's telling, then, "the poor" may have been "treated and despised as if they were beings of quite a different creation" (223), but they were not all the same, nor as deserving of that treatment. Some were good, honest, and well-doing, and some turbulent and indifferent. Some had more food than others, some more leverage with shopkeepers or members of their local relief committee, and some were less restrained by the values of their own people. Hence, some took soup, some used "influence" to get onto the public works, and, more commonly, some denied others the charity demanded by custom. Like Levi, Dorian makes much of the absence of solidarity among "companions in misfortune". "Friendship was forgotten", he writes, and "men lived as if they dreaded each other, every one trying to do best for himself alone, and a man would rather deny the goods he possessed than make it known that he had such" (230). And an old man with food sufficient for himself but not to share with his grandchild becomes himself a figure of pity (214–15).

If there is sympathy for a man who could feed himself but not his family, there is none for those who sought to profit at the expense of their companions in misfortune. "The landlords are often accused, and justly so, for their oppression, cruelty and tyranny, but unfortunately a man's very neighbour is very often just as pitiless a tyrant". It is the grabber who is Dorian's great bête noire (191–2).[24] The bailiffs who enabled the grabbers might have been "men chosen from the lowest scum of society, unscrupulous, unmerciful beings", but, in Dorian's mind, at least some of them – eager for revenge, and imitative of the master, easily bought with food or drink – can be understood, for their weaknesses are "human":

*'Tis true most of the bum bailiffs were always of the lowest type of humanity, but a few were constrained to accept of this miserable occupation urged by the thought of the oppression or cruelty exercised towards themselves or relatives a short time before, so that there was therefore a grudge and no way to exercise it but by this stroke of getting under the protection of the landlord and having the power at their back; the farmer who thought so little of getting a cabin lowered, found to his grief, that though he had crushed, yet he did not kill the worm, and that the one he thought as little of was now in a position to persecute and torment him*

*and ultimately turn him out. If former cruelty be any palliation for a spirit of revenge, it is to be feared that some kept it in view. Such is humankind and the time is yet to arrive when men will forget injury and for the same return good* (239).

But the grabbers themselves are consumed by inhuman greed. And in his repeated insistence on their extraordinary avarice – "The greedy man thinks deeply, his eyes see far" (a rendering of the Irish proverb *Tchí saint i bhfad*, Greed sees far) (191) – he may hit on a rule of famine: in times of great dearth it is the "greedy" among the poor – the first to break customary obligations to share – who may be most likely to prevail. Tellingly, in elaborating what happened in his own community, Dorian juxtaposes the rise of the grabbers – among them "those who might be called the lower class" – with the drifting downwards of "the 'genteel folk' ... unwilling to make any narrow shift or to be seen connected with any mean action" (227–9). And if here Dorian anticipates Levi's apprehension that "the worst ... the selfish, the violent, the insensitive, the collaborators" sometimes predominate among the saved, then his own callous attitude towards the disappearance of "turbulent and indifferent" neighbors may be taken as proof of it.

\*

Hugh Dorian died in an overcrowded house on Nelson Street in Derry's Bogside, and he has lain in an unmarked grave in Derry City Cemetery since 1914. The city of Derry will never raise a monument to him. And, indeed, what stone could speak of a man indifferent to the loss of "many" of his neighbors? But Dorian's testimony is exceptional. Nobody from a lower tier of society put down on paper a more complete ground-level account of the horror that made modern Ireland. Still, the words of other Famine survivors did echo into the middle decades of the twentieth century, most obviously from the 1930s to the 1960s, when people born within a few decades of the Famine were asked by collectors of the Irish Folklore Commission (IFC) what they had heard from their parents of *am an drochshaoil* (the time of the bad life). In response, they told stories of thievery, hoarding, land-grabbing, meal-mongering, and moneylending. Sometimes, indeed, they put names to "obscene and pathetic figures" in their own communities – people whose descendants were living beside them – and time and again they picked over situations where, in the end, judgement is best suspended. Scenes at the Famine pot loomed large in *seanchas* (oral history). For instance, in Rann na Feirste, west Donegal, Séamas Ó Dónaill, born about 1858, recalled hearing that when a pot or boiler for making broth was set up in the second year of the Famine, two local women charged with doling out the rations skimmed the thin gruel at the top for the hungry and kept for themselves the thicker, more nutritious *gríodar* at the bottom.

*Is iomaí lá garbh a bhí ag an choire chéanna. Bhí na daoine chomh hocrach agus nár fhan truaighe nó grásta ar bith iontu ...* (Póirtéir 69) *[There were many rough days at the same pot. The people were that hungry that they became devoid of pity and grace. A strong man would drive women, children, and weak ones out of his road. They used to be tramping on top of each other, everybody trying to get to the pot.*

*A poor man came to the pot one day, and he stood apart from the crowd for a while. There were that many people gathered around it that a woman fainted. A way was cleared, and two men took her out from the pot, and threw her on the ground behind the crowd. They then tried to get back to the pot, not caring if the woman died or not. There, they found the poor fellow standing at the pot where the woman had been. One of them grabbed him by the throat, and threw him on the back of his head on a pile of stones.*

*"It is little enough would make me take you, and shove you into the pot," he said to the poor man, "To think that you'd come to drink our broth, that is scarce enough – too scarce – for ourselves."*

*The poor man got up, and he walked away without saying a single word.*

*There was a man called Eoghan Thuathail at the pot, and he had been watching all that happened, and it stung him to see the abuse given the poor man. He called him back, and he gave him half of his broth.]* [my translation].

\*

On January 3, 1847 eleven of fourteen people buried in Kilmoe churchyard in west Cork were interred "without other covering than the rags they wore when alive". "The distress is so appalling", a "gentleman" considered "good and charitable" remarked on hearing of those burials, "that we must throw away all feelings of delicacy".[25] Neither the "survivor's account" that is Dorian's narrative nor *seanchas* collected from the generation that succeeded him is entirely free of "delicacy". Dorian nowhere identifies as Fánaid the community of which he writes; nor does he give the actual name of any individual in it. And, as for *seanchas*, Séamas Ó Dónaill – who told that story of the riot in Rann na Feirste – avoided mentioning the names of the women doling out the broth. The economist Cormac Ó Gráda, while insisting on the value of *seanchas* for the history of the Famine, observes that IFC respondents had a tendency to represent their own locality as having fared better in the late 1840s than surrounding ones. It was also relatively uncommon for respondents to name individuals who perished of starvation or disease; likewise, "accusatory stories" about land-grabbers and meal-mongers tended to be told without identifying the offending families. And these tendencies to gloss over subjects that might provoke shame or guilt, Ó Gráda argues, have left "open the way for a version of famine history in which the descendants of those who survived all become vicarious victims" (*Black '47* 194–225).[26] The avaricious and the usurious have faded from view, then, as has the family that closed the door on the person in need who was subsequently found dead in a ditch.

**Figure 8** | Anon. *Portrait of Cardinal Paul Cullen*

# EMERGENCE

During a famine in Algeria in 1868, Archbishop Charles Lavigerie endeavored to convert Islamic orphans to Catholicism. Fearing that proselytism might provoke unrest, Marshal Patrice de MacMahon, then governor of the colony (and later president of France), resisted these efforts, and he rebuked Lavigerie for imputing cases of cannibalism to Islam: "You will doubtless admit with me that Ireland is one of the most religious countries in the world. Nevertheless, during the last famine cases of cannibalism occurred there as well as now in Algeria." On reading MacMahon's remarks, Cardinal Paul Cullen [Figure 8] of Dublin took it upon himself to write to *L'Univers*, a strident ultramontane newspaper, and *Le Monde Illustré* to refute the suggestion that Irish people had consumed human flesh in the 1840s:

*As soon as my attention was called to these words, I thought it my duty to inquire whether there was any foundation for the statement they contain; and I have learned from the best authorities that not one single instance of cannibalism occurred in Ireland during the long years of a famine with which it was lately desolated, and that the country remained altogether free from those awful scenes of violence and murder which the followers of the Koran have perpetrated in Algiers within the last few months. The famine, indeed, was most severe, and of long duration, in Ireland, and poor people had to undergo suffering almost unparalleled in the annals of the world; but, in the midst of their trials, the true religion of Christ and the maxims of the gospel inspired them with patience and resignation, and they invariably prepared to encounter the horrors of starvation by approaching the sacraments of penance and the Holy Eucharist. Far from laying violent hands on their fellow creatures, or endeavouring to preserve their own lives at the expense of the blood of others and even of their own children, as has happened among the Mahometans in Algeria, the poor Irish Catholics in thousands of instances are known to have divided their last morsel of bread with their fellow sufferers; and it is recorded of many parents that, though dying themselves of hunger, they abstained from touching the last remnants of food in their possession, in order, if possible, to preserve the lives of their children.[27]*

Cullen's letter, although addressed, in the first instance, to French newspapers, was widely reproduced in the Irish press, and it served his domestic political purposes. Irish Catholics, *in extremis*, had been devoted to their faith and attended to their priests; they had not laid "violent hands on their fellow creatures", and, in 1868, Catholics would do well to take their clergymen's advice – that is, give short shrift to Fenians, who, a year earlier, had staged an insurrection with a view to establishing a republic.

Three misrepresentations of the recent past are central to Cullen's letter.[28] His claim that there had been no cannibalism in the late 1840s was untrue. In an insightful study, Cormac Ó Gráda establishes that, while the taboo against cannibalism (or what the Cork gentleman termed "delicacy") may have inhibited the press from reporting it, a few incidents garnered attention. Ó Gráda discusses two. Both occurred in west Connemara, one in 1848 and the other in 1849: the first involved the wife of John Connelly of Kilkerrin, near Clifden, who – a magistrate told her husband's trial for sheep stealing in March 1848 – ate the legs of her own dead child; the second concerned Patrick Diamond, from Claggan, near Clifden, who was reported to have eaten the liver of a shipwrecked sailor. And Ó Gráda notes that the parish priest of Spiddal, also in Connemara, wrote of the latter incident, which was raised at Westminster, that it was "a tale, alas, too familiar here" (*Eating People is Wrong* 35-6).[29] There were other cases. In March 1847 the *Southern Reporter* described how, in a hovel in or near Ratooragh, west Cork, some men employed on public works found the bodies of a father and son; the father's hand was in the son's mouth, and he had gnawed three of the fingers. "It is our duty to publish these appalling facts", remarked the editor, adding "We have authentic information of others just as dreadful, but our flesh creeps at the remembrance; we cannot go on with the relation."[30] Similarly, in August 1849 Peter Ward, parish priest of Partry, County Mayo, detailed instances of cannibalism in an appeal to the Central Relief Committee; he was prepared, he wrote, to swear to the facts on oath:

*In the village of Drimcaggy four were dead together in a poor hut – brother, two sisters, and daughter. The flesh was torn off the daughter's arm and mangled in the mouth of her poor dead mother – her name was Mary Kennedy. William Walsh, of Mount Partree, and his son were dead together, their flesh was torn off their dead bodies by rats, and by each other; flesh was found in their mouths. His wife and child died the week before of hunger. Patt Shaughnessy declared that, such was the agony of hunger that he would eat his own child unless relieved. He and his child died the same night together with his wife. These are true facts.*[31]

And so there was cannibalism in Cork, Galway, and Mayo in 1847–49. More cases may yet come to light. Still, the fact of cannibalism seems less significant than the idea of it – that is, for a period of three years many people in Ireland had been so reduced that it was conceivable they would eat human flesh. For instance, from late 1846, as hunger bit, disease spread, and mortality mounted, commentators returned time and again to the animal food that people had been reduced to eating – horse beans, a distempered cow, a putrid pig, a foal, a dog, a donkey, water cress, nettles, grass – and also to the breakdown of traditional mortuary practices, most especially the burial of the dead without shroud or coffin. And, in all four provinces, they wrote with shock and horror of seeing the dead being left unburied, becoming carrion fed on by dogs, pigs, rats, ravens, and gulls.

Shock is understandable. As Thomas W. Laqueur argues in his absorbing history of mortal remains, the dead throughout human history have been used to make social worlds: "They define generations, demarcate the sacred and the profane and more ordinary spaces as well, are the guarantors of land and power and authority, mirror the living to themselves, and insist on our temporal limits." Hence, the brutal disposal or, indeed, discarding of corpses constitutes an act of extreme violence, a denial of the very humanity of the deceased (1–4). And, with dogs and pigs ravaging corpses – the great fear of the Widow Keating – the civilizational wall prohibiting people from consuming human flesh was falling. Certainly, in February 1848, when John MacHale, archbishop of Tuam (and sometime opponent of Cullen), described how "dogs are seen devouring the dead, and the living, in return, killing and feeding on the dogs", the spectre of cannibalism was very close.[32] The Connelly case, in which the woman consumed the flesh of her own child, had likely by this stage occurred in Clifden, part of MacHale's archdiocese, and it would soon be mentioned in the press.

Also a misrepresentation was Cullen's insinuation that the starving Catholic poor had all cleaved to the Church. Attendance at weekly Mass was a canonical obligation for Catholics; however, a survey in 1834 showed that only about forty-three per cent of Irish Catholics were fulfilling it, with attendance levels significantly lower in Irish-speaking districts in the west (Miller 90–106).[33] Admittedly, even lax Catholics considered extreme unction (the last rites) important, and Cullen was explicitly referring to it. Yet his letter, which concluded by praising the French newspapers for supporting "the Rights of the Holy See and Catholic education", conjures a chapel-focused piety that was not common among the Irish poor of the 1840s. An exchange at the first, abandoned, trial of Johnny Finn, the child charged with killing the Donoghues, illuminated the relative indifference of the poor to chapel-centered devotions. A defense attorney asked fourteen-year-old Johnny Donoghue, the brother of the murdered children, if he understood the meaning of an oath – he did not – and the judge then followed with questions intended to establish if he could tell right from wrong:

*Were you ever at a church or chapel?*
*No, sir*
*Was your mother ever there?*
*Yes, sir.*
*Did she ever take you there?*
*No, sir.*

Figure 9 | Michael Davitt

*Did you ever hear of heaven or hell?*
*No, sir.*
*Did you ever hear of God?*
*No, sir.*

An attorney then asked if the boy (who lived about three miles from Drinagh chapel) knew what would become of him if he told a lie, and he replied that he did not.[34] Of course, mass mortality in the years of the Famine reaped a swathe of that underclass, as, too, did mass migration, and by 1868, when Cullen wrote, continued migration and less and later marriage had further depleted the remnants of it. Meanwhile, the Church – through the access to children accorded to it by the new National schools – bedded down in the 1840s and 1850s, and, helped by the shock-and-awe tactics of the Redemptorists and other missionary orders, was orienting poorer Catholics to chapel. The poor increasingly were the very type of people that Cullen imagined to have died of hunger and disease; it was becoming easy to forget the actual lives of the Famine dead.

Finally, Cullen's claim that the Irish had been passive during the Famine was a misrepresentation: after the recurrence of blight in 1846, the poor held massive demonstrations demanding employment to enable them to purchase food; they rioted to secure foodstuffs, "pirated" ships laden with Indian meal off the coast, and plundered convoys of carts transporting flour **[Figure 11]**. For sure, many observers remarked on apathy, indifference, dejection, and despondency spreading among the lower classes – common features of famine – and the scale and frequency of protest did decline in the latter years of the crisis – that is, after 1848; still, even then, evicting bailiffs, tenants clearing subtenants, poor-rate collectors, and process servers distraining stock or crops met resistance.[35] Paradoxically, the notion that the starving had been passive was also an article of faith for Cullen's bêtes noires, the Fenians; but, contra Cullen, they deplored it. For Michael Davitt **[Figure 9]**, a Fenian, who from 1879 was a land activist, the Famine dead were "slaves ... who died like sheep, without leaving on record one single redeeming trait of courageous manhood to the credit of their memories".

*There is possibly no chapter in the wide records of human suffering and wrong so full*
*of shame – measureless, unadulterated, sickening shame – as that which tells us of (it is*
*estimated) a million of people including, presumably, two hundred thousand adult men, lying*
*down to die in a land out of which forty-five millions' worth of food was being exported, in*
*one year alone, for rent – the product of their own toil – and making no effort, combined or*
*otherwise, to assert even the animal's right of existence – the right to live by the necessities of*
*its nature. It stands unparalleled in human history, nothing approaching to it in the complete*
*surrender of all the ordinary attributes of manhood by almost a whole nation, in the face of*
*an artificial famine (47–8).[36]*

Davitt, there writing in his *Fall of Feudalism* (1904), was trying to use the dead for political purposes – that is, to use their fate to stir people to activism. He had done so many times before. Indeed, representing the Famine dead as people who never resisted was a central rhetorical strategy in one of his most powerful speeches, an emotive oration delivered to a crowd put at twenty thousand by some reporters, in his birthplace, Straide, County Mayo on February 1, 1880. Standing on a platform erected on the very site of the house from which his family had been evicted in September 1850 and which he, as a child of four, had watched being "burned down by agents of the landlord, assisted by agents of the law", and conscious, too, that "in the memory of many now listening to my words" the then depopulated district had once been loud with the laughter of children, he had stressed that "every nerve would have to be strained to stave off, if possible, the horrible fate which befell our famine-slaughtered kindred in 1847 and 1848". He had grown up, he said, in "a strange land", listening to "accounts of famine and sorrow, of deaths from landlordism, of coffinless graves", of scenes

> *On highway's side, where oft were seen*
> *The wild dog and the vulture keen*
> *Tug for the limbs and gnaw the face*
> *Of some starved child of our Irish race.*

And he proceeded to deplore the "abrogation of our manhood" in those years, and how smallholders "stood by like a flock of frightened sheep, timid and terrified, unable to prevent this human bird of prey [the landlord] from devouring their own and their children's substance".[37]

As a rhetorical strategy, summoning up the Famine dead had clear potential for land reformers and republicans: the British state was responsible for the outworking of the crisis, and landlords had grasped the opportunity afforded by the Irish Poor Law Extension Act of 1847 to get rid of tenants (and to get tenants to get rid of subtenants). "Extermination" – the term applied to Famine evictions in the liberal and nationalist press (and in Dorian's narrative) – is not an inappropriate description of the consequences of the Act's notorious Gregory, or quarter-acre, clause for tens of thousands of poor families. Yet, no less than Cullen's representation of a passive poor, whose faith had kept them from eating each other, Davitt's rhetoric required amnesia on the part of his audience. Many of those who had emerged from the gray zone of the Famine – not least, the land-grabber and meal-monger – had thrived through the 1850s, 1860s, and 1870s. In communities across Ireland there were families – including some shopkeeper-publicans who came to political prominence in the land agitations of the 1880s – that had not let the crisis go to waste.

People who allowed a corpse to remain so long on the road from Castlebar to Newport that, when removed for burial, in February 1848, it had "partly melted away", may have survived into the twentieth century.[38] So, too, may have

Figure 10 | Jeremiah O'Donovan Rossa, Mountjoy Prison, 1866

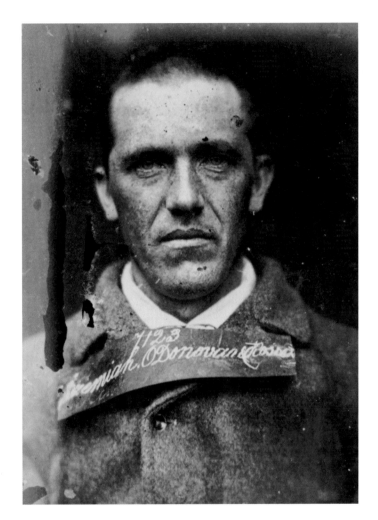

*Jerh. O'Donovan Rossa*

some tenants in Killeeneen, County Galway – among them Conneelys, Keanes, Killileas, and Rehills – who tumbled and burned a dozen houses belonging to their undertenants – all of whom were on outdoor relief – on a single day in June 1848.[39] And so may have three householders in Kilmactranny, County Sligo who, on a night in January 1847, refused to admit Thomas McManus because, they claimed, he was suffering from typhoid fever. A man who had found McManus in a muddy ditch had sought shelter for him at the three nearest houses, and, being thrice refused, had then carried him to a haggard and placed him on some straw; when found the following morning he was dead and both his legs had been eaten off to the buttocks by a pig. Those who saw the "agonized expression of M'Manus's countenance" reckoned that he had been alive when the pig attacked him. There was not so much as a "particle of food" found in his stomach or intestines during a post-mortem examination; the coroner returned a verdict of "death by hunger and cold", and made no mention of fever.[40]

Hugh Dorian, who was born *c.* 1834, died in Derry's Bogside in 1914. The following year Jeremiah O'Donovan Rossa **[Figure 10]** died in Staten Island, New York. He had been born in 1831 in Reenascreena, near Rosscarbery, west Cork. A single townland – a few hundred yards – lay between it and Carhoogarriff, home to Johnny Finn, the boy who, when employed on the public works in March 1847, was alleged to have killed the Donoghue children for a bag of meal. That winter Rossa's own father, Denis, had been working as a ganger on the public works, making a new road through Rowry Glen. However, he had taken ill, and the fifteen-year-old Rossa had been given his place; he was on the works on March 25 when word came that he was wanted at home, and there he learned that his father had died. Shortly before his father's death, Rossa's mother, Nellie, had gone to her sister-in-law's house to ask for help. There, she overheard that woman's son-in-law say that "we [Rossa's family] were so far in debt, and the children so young and helpless, that anything given us or spent on us to get us over the present difficulty would only be lost, lost forever; and that then we would not be over the difficulty." Now, on Denis's death, creditors came looking for their money, and there being no money, a man named Bill Ned obtained decrees against them. And in May 1847 Rossa saw their furniture removed from their house and auctioned on the street. A notice of eviction was then served on the family by the land agent, Garrett Barry. "The agent", he remembered, "was a cousin of ours, and he told my mother that it was better for her to give up the land quietly, and he would do all he could to help her." Courtesy of Barry, the family remained on in another house in Reenascreena, until late 1848, when Rossa's brother (who an uncle had taken out to Philadelphia after the family's eviction) paid the passage to America for his mother, brother, and sister (O'Donovan Rossa 108–40).[41]

Rossa himself was by then living in Skibbereen, working as a clerk in a relative's shop. The Keatings of Letter were all dead. But he got to know Jerry Crowley, the apothecary who helped Daniel Donovan to bury the seven-year-old boy in the kitchen garden. It was in Crowley's shop that, in 1856, Rossa established the Phoenix

National and Literary Society, a group later absorbed by the Fenians (O'Donovan Rossa 179–84).[42] And when Crowley died in January 1857, Rossa composed a long epitaph that describes his coffin being carried to the Abbeystrewry churchyard:

> ...
>
> *Skibbereen now mourns his spirit fled,*
> *For Doctor Jerrie Crowley's dead.*
> *Each hill from Skea to Clashatarbh,*
> *Cries out "Ta Dochtuir Jerrie marbh."*
>
> ...
>
> *A hearse next day its presence showed*
> *To take him to his last abode,*
> *Brought forth amid an ullagone,*
> *The public claimed him as their own,*
> *And said no hearse should bear his weight,*
> *From thence unto the Abbey gate* (O'Donovan Rossa 180–2).[43]

Rossa also knew Dr Donovan, the compassionate chronicler of famine mortality and the social and "moral" collapse that attends it; Donovan's mother had been his family's landlord in Reenascreena. A "middle-tenant", holding land under Lord Carbery, it was she who had evicted Rossa's own widowed mother in summer 1847 (O'Donovan Rossa 94–6).

Rossa became, like Davitt, a Fenian. In 1858–59 he was imprisoned without trial for seven months for his political activities. Convicted of high treason in 1865, he endured a brutal regime in English prisons until, in 1870, he was released under an amnesty and exiled to America. There, he was once a guest in Tom Curley's hotel in Troy, New York. Curley was a native of Ballinasloe, County Galway – a place, like Skibbereen, where the poor had been obliterated in the late 1840s. The two men fell to talking of "the bad times", and Curley asked him had he ever "felt the hunger". "I told him I did not", Rossa later wrote,

*but that I had felt something that was worse than the hunger; that I felt it still; and that was – the degradation into which want and hunger will reduce human nature. I told him of that Sunday evening in Ross when I went home to my dinner, and my mother had no dinner for me; I told him how I had one penny piece in my pocket; I told him how I went out and bought for it a penny bun, and how I stole to the back of the house and thievishly ate that penny bun without sharing it with my mother and my sister and my brothers. I am proud of my life, one way or another; but that penny bun is a thorn in my side; a thorn in the pride of my life; it was only four ounces of bread – for bread was fourpence (eight cents) a pound at the time – but if I ever feel any pride in myself, that little loaf comes before me to humble me; it also comes before me to strengthen me in the determination to destroy that tyranny that reduces my people to poverty and degradation, and makes them what it is not natural for them to be. I know it is not in my nature to be niggardly and selfish. I know that if I have money above my wants, I find more happiness and satisfaction in giving it to friends who want it than in keeping it. But that penny-bun affair clashes altogether against my own measurement of myself, and stands before me like a ghost whenever I would think of raising myself in my own estimation. I suppose it was the general terror and alarm of starvation that was around me at the time that paralyzed my nature, and made me do what I am now ashamed to say I did* (122–3).

Eaten bread that was never forgotten. Primo Levi understood that shame. Few survivors of the *Lagers*, he wrote, felt guilty "about having deliberately damaged, robbed, or beaten a companion", but "almost everybody" felt guilty at having omitted to offer help, that is, "of having failed in terms of human solidarity".

*The presence at your side of a weaker – or less cunning, or older, or too young – companion, hounding you with his demands for help or with his simple presence, in itself an entreaty, is a constant in the life of the Lager. The demand for solidarity, for a human word, advice, even just a listening ear, was permanent and universal but rarely satisfied. There was no time, space, privacy, patience, strength; most often, the person to whom the request was addressed found himself in his turn in a state of need, entitled to comfort* (78).

An incident in August 1944 remained in Levi's memory. It had been hot that month in Auschwitz and water had been in short supply. One day he had discovered a liter of stagnant water, trapped in a pipe, and he had shared it, secretly, slyly, with only one friend rather than with his entire work squad. Later, when he had encountered another member of the squad, gray with cement dust and his lips cracked, Levi had felt guilty. That fellow had realized what the other two had done, and, years later, he could ask, "Why the two of you and not I?" And whenever they met, "the veil of that act of omission, that unshared glass of water, stood between us, transparent, not expressed, but perceptible and 'costly'" (79–81).

Levi acknowledges that he and others who survived the Holocaust and wrote of it had, in one way or another, won "a position of privilege":

*We who were favored by fate tried, with more or less wisdom, to recount not only our own fate but that of the others, indeed of the drowned; but this was a discourse "on behalf of third parties", the story of things seen at close hand, not experienced personally. The destruction brought to an end, the job completed, was not told by anyone, just as no one ever returned to describe his own death* (84).

As mentioned, Rossa's people, through the favor of their cousin, the land agent, remained for a period in a house in Reenascreena where one of their subtenants had formerly lived. And, in 1851, Hugh Dorian – likely through the intervention of a priest – became a schoolmaster, a salaried employee of the Board of Education (Dorian 27). They, too, in these and other respects, not least their literacy, were in "positions of privilege", and it is important to keep sight of those positions when reading their narratives. To repeat, Dorian decried the injustice of government ("the successful blow – and it would appear premeditated – the great blow for slowly taking away human life, getting rid of the people and nothing else ... next to slow murder") and landlords ("extermination"); and he denounced the land-grabbers and meal-mongers that thrived in the 1840s when established moral codes were abandoned. But he shed no tears for the "turbulent and indifferent persons and characters who were only a disgrace to the good, the honest, and the well-doing". Tellingly, in his narrative one detects the same shame at not sharing that stayed with Rossa (and Levi), but it is, almost slyly, projected onto others:

*It came to this that even the few who had some worldly substance about them were afraid to own it and were afraid to use it except under pressing necessity, and not only that but the persons who had sufficient nourishment in food showed signs as if it did them no good. This in a sense was not to be wondered at, as it could not be otherwise to a man of feeling, knowing that his neighbour, his friend, or a near relative, perhaps his grandchild, was without food and was hungry* (214–15).

And shame lightly shadows the closing of Dorian's narrative, when he recollects people who had survived the Famine meeting in later years:

*Their conversations then were not as in the years long and not long past – not of wars, not of battles, nor the strength of nations; no, their subjects were lacking words, more silent, [and of a] more mournful nature.*

*It was a rehearsal of their own sad experience of the past few years – the silence, the sadness, the desolation around, caused by the Famine, by the crowbar brigade, and by emigration; of the death of many of their near acquaintances, who were hurried away in a short time ... the recollection of the immense population at one time, and their dispersion almost unawares* (323).

Still, the shadows flit and fade as he skips to the time of writing, 1890, and marvels at children having "all the requisites desirable" for education: "the manager's rules; the teacher's time table; the teacher's competency; the monitors with pointers in their hands watching over and keeping classes in subjection ... books, slates, pencils, chalk, pen, ink, paper, and so forth". The implicit contrast is with his own childhood, before the Famine, when the few "scholars" in his district went to ill-equipped hedge schools or to establishments managed by proselytizing evangelicals (323–4). And there, in his remembrance of subjects "lacking words" and his insistence that better times had come and that still better times were yet to come, one hears the voice of a resilient man.

But then people are resilient – even those who, having avoided the abyss, feel ashamed of what they did not do for others, of their failure, when themselves reduced, to have offered human solidarity.[44]

**FOOD RIOT IN DUNGARVON.**
(Etched and cast in relief by the Glyphographic Process.)

People who lived through the Famine were conscious of subjects "lacking words", things about which it was hard to talk: the dog eaten, the charity denied the widow, who then died, the corpse devoured by dogs. Still, narratives like those of Dorian and Rossa and, indeed, stories told by the generation that came after them give the lie to the facile notion, popularized in the 1990s, that the Famine was "so deeply tragic as to be too traumatic to recall".[45]

Stories told of the Famine have served political purposes. Certainly, they have given force to arguments for Irish independence; and how could they not, when, in the most benign version of events, the horror unfolded on the British government's watch? But those stories also speak to what it means to be human. And now, in our time of widening inequality and environmental collapse, the "reduction" of Irish people by hunger and disease in the late 1840s may yet, like that stone which Daniel Donovan proposed to raise over the Widow Keating, "draw a pitying tear" for the living no less than for the dead.

**Figure 11** | "**Food Riot in Dungarvon [sic]**" (*Pictorial Times*, October 10, 1846)

# ENDNOTES

[1] "Distress in west Carbery. Diary of a dispensary doctor", *Southern Reporter*, January 26, 1847. The *Cork Examiner*, January 25, 1847, includes an extract from a letter by Crowley describing the incident; a printer's error, misidentifying the townland as South Reen, was corrected on January 29.

[2] *Southern Reporter*, February 13, 1847. The couplet is adapted from *Dione. A Pastoral Tragedy*, Act V, scene iii, by John Gay (1685–1732).

[3] See esp. 148–9. The estimate of the death toll in the medical profession was made, in 1848, by James William Cusack and William Stokes; for a critique by three other prominent doctors, see National Archives of Ireland (hereafter NAI), Official Papers Series II, 1848/317, Central Board of Health, Dublin, Report of Commissioners, viz. Sir Philip Crampton, Sir H. Marsh and Dr Corrigan, rel. to charges made against the Govt. and Board of Health.

[4] From the second part of "Observations on the peculiar diseases to which the famine of last year gave origin and on the morbid effects of insufficient nourishment", published in three parts in *Dublin Medical Press*, February 2, 1848 (starvation), March 1, 1848 (fever), and May 3, 1848 (dysentery).

[5] *Census of Ireland 1851: Part I ..., County of Cork (W. Riding)*, HC 1852–53 (1551), XCI.499, 138.

[6] *Downpatrick Recorder*, March 13, 1847; *Newry Telegraph*, March 13, 1847; *Galway Vindicator*, March 20, 1847.

[7] *Tralee Chronicle*, February 20, 1847.

[8] On the killings, see the first trial of Finn, in *Cork Examiner*, April 5, 1848, and also his second trial, in *Cork Examiner*, July 31, 1848.

[9] NAI, Outrage Papers, 1847/6/485, Union Hall, Rosscarbery, March 12, 1847, Somerville to Redington, enclosing a copy of Johnny Finn's confession, dated March 12, 1847.

[10] *Cork Examiner*, July 31, 1848; *Dublin Evening Packet*, July 29, 1848.

[11] *Dublin Medical Press*, February 2, 1848.

[12] *The Primary Valuation of Ireland* (Griffith's Valuation), 1848–64.

[13] *Cork Examiner*, July 13, 1849.

[14] *Dublin Evening Packet*, April 17, 1847. For the acquittal of her killer, see *Mayo Constitution*, August 8, 1848.

[15] NAI, Outrage Papers, 1847/21/317, Castlebar, April 22, 1847, Atkinson to Redington. See also *Dublin Evening Packet*, April 24, 1847.

[16] Letter of Enright to Dr Cornelius Egan, in *Cork Examiner*, February 22, 1847.

[17] *Kerry Examiner*, January 19, 1847.

[18] *Southern Reporter*, January 26, 1847.

[19] *Dublin Medical Press*, February 2, 1848.

[20] For a discussion of why mortal remains matter that takes Diogenes's remarks as its starting point, see Laqueur, *The Work of the Dead*.

[21] For works on the Famine that reference Levi's memoirs, see Kelleher, *The Feminization of Famine*, and Gibbons, "Words upon the windowpane", 43–56. Joe Lee draws on what "we know from other horrible human experiences, not least the Holocaust", in "Famine as history", 159–75, esp. 167–9, 172.

[22] On cannibalism, see Ó Gráda, *Eating People is Wrong*, 11–37, esp. 30–6.

[23] My emphasis. Elsewhere, discussing the work demanded of the hungry by members of relief committees, Dorian remarks, "All this circuitous way of doing good was more like hard labour or convict punishment" (222).

[24] See also 228-9, 239-40, *et seq.*

[25] From an editorial in *Cork Examiner*, January 8, 1847. The gentleman was Daniel McCarthy of Skibbereen.

[26] See esp. 203-6, 210-11. See also Ó Gráda, "Famine, trauma and memory", 217-33.

[27] *Evening Freeman*, June 8, 1868.

[28] Cullen was a native of Kildare, a county estimated by Joel Mokyr to have had the sixth lowest rate of excess mortality (lower-bound estimate) in Ireland in 1846-51. See his *Why Ireland Starved: A Quantitative and Analytical History of the Irish Economy, 1800-1850* (London: George Allen and Unwin, 1983), 267. The data are reproduced in a useful table and graph in James S. Donnelly Jr., *The Great Irish Potato Famine* (Stroud: Sutton Publishing, 2001), 176-7.

[29] The primary source for the Connelly case is *Galway Vindicator*, April 1, 1848.

[30] *Southern Reporter*, March 23, 1847.

[31] *Dublin Evening Packet*, August 21, 1849.

[32] *Freeman's Journal*, February 19, 1848.

[33] See esp. 96-7, and works cited therein.

[34] *Cork Examiner*, April 5, 1848.

[35] On crime and protest in famine, see Ó Gráda, *Famine: A Short History*, 52-6. For the Irish case, see Eiríksson, "Food supply and food riots".

[36] For a discussion, see "Introduction", in Delaney and Mac Suibhne, eds, *Ireland's Great Famine and Popular Politics*, 1-9.

[37] For Davitt's recollection of the speech, see his *The Fall of Feudalism in Ireland*, 202-3. For newspaper reports, see *Freeman's Journal*, February 2, February 3, 1880.

[38] *Dublin Evening Packet*, February 19, 1848.

[39] NAI, Outrage Papers, 1848/11/565, Craughwell, June 28, 1848, Lynch to Redington, enclosing statements of evicted undertenants.

[40] *Sligo Champion*, January 16, 1847.

[41] On O'Donovan Rossa, see Kenna, *Jeremiah O'Donovan Rossa*.

[42] On O'Donovan Rossa's death, see *Cork Examiner*, February 4, 1857.

[43] "Doctor Jerrie Crowley", in O'Donovan Rossa, *Rossa's Recollections*, 180-2; *ullagone*, English orthography for Irish *olagón*, lamentation; *T[á] Docht[ú]ir Jerrie marbh*, Doctor Jerry is dead.

[44] On psychological resilience, see Ó Ciosáin, "Famine memory", 95-117.

[45] Michael D. Higgins, president of Ireland, on a state visit to Cuba, quoted in the *Irish Times*, February 18, 2017. For critiques of this idea, see Ó Ciosáin, "Famine memory", 96-8, 112-14, Ó Gráda, "Famine, trauma and memory", 228-33, and Beiner, 'Memory too has a history'.

# WORKS CITED

Beiner, Guy. "Memory too has a history". *Dublin Review of Books* (March 2015). http://www.drb.ie/essays/memory-too-has-a-history (accessed March 23, 2017).

Davitt, Michael. *The Fall of Feudalism in Ireland, or the Story of the Land League Revolution*. London & New York: Harper & Brothers Publishers, 1904.

Delaney, Enda and Breandán Mac Suibhne, eds. *Ireland's Great Famine and Popular Politics*. New York: Routledge, 2016.

Donnelly Jr., James S. *The Great Irish Potato Famine*. Stroud: Sutton Publishing, 2001.

Dorian, Hugh. *The Outer Edge of Ulster: A Memoir of Social Life in Nineteenth-century Donegal*. Eds. Breandán Mac Suibhne and David Dickson. Dublin: Lilliput, 2000; Notre Dame: University of Notre Dame Press, 2001.

Eiríksson, Andrés. "Food supply and food riots". In Cormac Ó Gráda, ed. *Famine 150: Commemorative Lecture Series*. Dublin: Teagasc and UCD, 1997.

Gibbons, Luke. "Words upon the windowpane: image, text, and Irish culture". In James Elkins, ed. *Visual Cultures*. Chicago: University of Chicago Press, 2010.

Kelleher, Margaret. *The Feminization of Famine: Expressions of the Inexpressible*. Cork: Cork University Press, 1997.

Kenna, Shane. *Jeremiah O'Donovan Rossa: Unrepentant Fenian*. Dublin: Merrion Press, 2015.

Laqueur, Thomas W. *The Work of the Dead: A Cultural History of Mortal Remains*. Princeton, NJ: Princeton University Press, 2015.

Lee, Joe. "Famine as history". In Cormac Ó Gráda, ed. *Famine 150: Commemorative Lecture Series*. Dublin: Teagasc and UCD, 1997.

Levi, Primo. *The Drowned and the Saved*. Trans. Raymond Rosenthal. New York: Vintage International, 1989.

Mokyr, Joel. *Why Ireland Starved: A Quantitative and Analytical History of the Irish Economy, 1800–1850*. London: George Allen and Unwin, 1983.

Ó Ciosáin, Niall. "Famine memory and the popular representation of scarcity". In Ian McBride, ed. *History and Memory in Modern Ireland*. Cambridge: Cambridge University Press, 2001.

O'Donovan Rossa, Jeremiah. *Rossa's Recollections, 1838 to 1898. Memoirs of an Irish Revolutionary* [1898]. Intro. Seán Ó Lúing. Shannon: Irish University Press, 1972.

Ó Gráda, Cormac. *Black '47 and Beyond: The Great Irish Famine in History, Economy, and Memory*. Princeton, NJ: Princeton University Press, 1999.

---. "Famine, trauma and memory". In Cormac Ó Gráda, ed. *Ireland's Great Famine: Interdisciplinary Perspectives*. Dublin: University College Dublin Press, 2006.

---. *Famine: A Short History*. Princeton, NJ: Princeton University Press, 2009.

---. *Eating People is Wrong and Other Essays*. Princeton, NJ: Princeton University Press, 2015.

# IMAGES

**Cover**

**Micheal Farrell**
1940–2000
*The Wounded Wonder*
1997–98
Hillier's medium and
charcoal on canvas
55 x 62 in (132 x 157.5 cm)
© The Estate of Micheal Farrell

**Figure 1**

**Irish School**
*Lest We Forget*
Oil on canvas
30 x 40 in (76.2 x 101.6 cm)
Image provided by Ireland's
Great Hunger Museum,
Quinnipiac University

**Figure 2**

**Micheal Farrell**
1940–2000
*Black '47*
1997
Hand-colored lithograph
22 x 24 in (55.9 x 61 cm)
© The Estate of Micheal Farrell

**Figure 3**

**Rowan Gillespie**
b. 1953
*Famine*
1997
Customs House Quay, Dublin
Bronze
78.7-98.4 in (200-250 cm)
© Rowan Gillespie

**Figure 4**

**James Mahony**
1810-59
**"Old Chapel-Lane"**
*Illustrated London News*
February 13, 1847
Image provided by Ireland's
Great Hunger Museum,
Quinnipiac University

**Figure 5**

**Image of confession of Johnny Finn**
National Archives of Ireland
Image provided by author

**Figure 6**

**Brian Maguire**
b. 1951
*The World is Full of Murder* [Detail]
1985
Acrylic on canvas
53 x 86 in (134.6 x 218.4 cm)
© Brian Maguire

**Figure 7**

**Hugh Dorian manuscript**
Courtesy of Hugh Casey

**Figure 8**

**Portrait of Cardinal Paul Cullen**
c. 1875
St. Patrick's College,
Drumcondra
Image courtesy of Four Court
Press

**Figure 9**

**Michael Davitt**
c. 1878
Irish Political Figures
Photographic Collection
Image Courtesy of the National
Library of Ireland

**Figure 10**

**JeremiahO'Donovan Rossa, Mountjoy Prison**
1866
Thomas A. Larcom Photograph
Collection
New York Public Library

**Figure 11**

**"Food Riot in Dungarvon [*sic*]"**
*Pictorial Times*
October 10, 1846
Image provided by Ireland's
Great Hunger Museum,
Quinnipiac University

## ACKNOWLEDGMENTS

Some of the research on which this Famine Folio is based was made possible by a National Endowment for the Humanities Fellowship, a Franklin Grant awarded by the American Philosophical Society, and an Irish American Cultural Institute/Centre for Irish Studies Fellowship in the National University of Ireland, Galway; I am deeply grateful to the staff of all these bodies. While in Galway I benefited greatly from conversations with faculty in History, Irish, and Political Science. The fellows and staff of both the Moore Institute and Centre for Irish Studies were a tremendous support and encouragement, as, too, were the librarians and staff of the Hardiman Library, particularly its Special Collections section. I also owe an immense debt of gratitude to Gregory O'Connor and Paddy Sarsfield of the National Archives of Ireland for being expert guides to the vast collections of mid-nineteenth-century correspondence in their care. And thanks to Kathryn Kozarits, Nóra Rose, and Sarah, who made our time in Galway such great fun.

# ABOUT THE AUTHOR

Breandán Mac Suibhne is associate professor of history at Centenary University, New Jersey. Among his recent publications are *The End of Outrage: Post-Famine Adjustment in Rural Ireland* (Oxford: Oxford University Press, 2017) and, as editor, with Enda Delaney, *Ireland's Great Famine and Popular Politics* (New York and London: Routledge, 2016). Mac Suibhne is also editor of two annotated editions: John Gamble, *Society and Manners in Early Nineteenth-century Ireland* (Dublin: Field Day, 2011), and, with David Dickson, Hugh Dorian, *The Outer Edge of Ulster: A Memoir of Social Life in Nineteenth-century Donegal* (Dublin: Lilliput, 2000; Notre Dame: University of Notre Dame Press, 2001). In 2005 he was a founding editor, with critic Seamus Deane, of *Field Day Review*, a journal of political and literary culture published in Dublin.

**IRELAND'S GREAT HUNGER** MUSEUM | QUINNIPIAC UNIVERSITY PRESS ©2017

**SERIES EDITOR**
Niamh O'Sullivan

**IMAGE RESEARCH**
Claire Puzarne

**DESIGN**
www.rachelfoleydesigns.com

**ACKNOWLEDGMENT**
Office of Public Affairs, Quinnipiac University

**PUBLISHER**
Quinnipiac University Press

**PRINTING**
GRAPHYCEMS

ISBN  978-0-9978374-7-6

**Ireland's Great Hunger** Museum
Quinnipiac University

3011 Whitney Avenue
Hamden, CT 06518-1908
203-582-6500

**www.ighm.org**